Let's Talk

Positive Affirmations for the Soul

Nicole Thomas

ISBN: 1545207755

ISBN 13: 9781545207758

Table of Contents

Preface

Ever think about the words you use on a daily basis? Ever wonder how your negative talk and self-judgmental words impact you? It doesn't take a genius to know or recognize how powerful our words are. Our words have the ability to destroy and heal. The sad part is that many people are kinder to others than they are to themselves. We can see the best in others but not ourselves. Our self-judgment is harsh. We compare ourselves to others and criticize ourselves even more.

We complain that our hair is too short or too long; our nose is too big or too small; our body is too slim or too big. Nothing is ever right. And no matter how hard you try, you just don't make the cut. You fall short, and you let the world know it. And you remind yourself of your shortcomings daily.

Sometimes you don't realize you have created a pattern of negative thinking and self-talk. It has become second nature. When people remind you to quiet your inner critic, you tell them that you're just being a realist—when deep inside, you're simply afraid to stand and accept your truth; the truth that you are still a person of value, with faults and all. When you fold a twenty-dollar bill or

1

crumple it in your pocket, the bill still has its value. The same for you. Life has a way of beating us down. Disappointments may have shaken us to our core. But we still have value. We still have worth.

Truth be told:

- You are greater than your circumstances.
- You are smarter than you think.
- You are loving and kind.
- You are beautiful.

Let's Talk: Positive Affirmations for the Soul, is book of positive affirmations designed to help you change your thoughts and the words you speak over your life. At the end of the book, there is a section for you to write your own affirmations. I encourage you to use this section to write affirmations that speak directly to your situation.

There is also a section for you to write thirty days of notes and reflections on how the affirmations have impacted your daily routine and lifestyle.

My hope is that you will find this book useful. And my wish is that your words always speak life. Let them caress the essence of your soul and bring you hope and peace in an often chaotic, unstable world.

Daily Prayer

Father, allow the words from my mouth to touch the ears of your heart. Allow me to remember my worth in you. Help me to see myself the way you see me: a loving, kind spirit of light.

Amen

1

My eyes are open to my inner beauty and the beauty in my surroundings.

2

I am beautiful on the inside and outside.

3

I am good enough.

4

Every challenge makes me stronger and wiser.

5

I open my ears and eyes to fully appreciate my present state.

6
I have a voice.

7

I am strong and speak up for myself.

8
I am loved.

9

I love my body.

10
I love my life.

11
I have joy.

12
My life is filled with joy and happiness.

13
I am filled with love and peace.

14
I release anger and bitterness.

15

I forgive everyone who has hurt me.

16
I forgive myself.

17
I cherish my life and the
lives of others.

18
I have stability in my life.

19
My life is stable.

20
My finances are in order.

21
I give freely and openly.

22

I support the growth and development of others.

23
I have an open heart.

24

I welcome love and
friendship in my life.

25
I am surrounded by loving friends and family.

26
I am surrounded by positive people.

27
I am positive.

28
I love where I live.

29
I love my family.

30
I love my friends.

31
I love my job.

32
I love my colleagues.

34
I love my town.

35
I love my community.

36
I am active in my community.

37
I am a change agent.

38
I am a doer.

39
I am healthy.

40
I take care of my mind and body.

41
I fill my mind with healthy
and positive thoughts.

42
I fill my body with healthy foods.

43
Positive people enter my life.

44
I am talented.

45
Good things happen to me.

46
I love God, and He loves me.

47
My future is bright.

Questions to Consider

1. Which affirmation resonated with you the most, and why?

   _____

   _____

   _____

   _____

2. Did you feel any different after saying the affirmations out loud? Explain.

   _____

   _____

   _____

   _____

3. Did you start doing things differently after saying the affirmations out loud? If yes, then what changes did you observe in your behavior?

_____

_____

_____

_____

4. Did saying the affirmations out loud impact your attitude? If yes, in what way?

_____

_____

_____

_____

5. Did the affirmations change the way you feel about yourself? Family? Friends? Community? If yes, explain the way your feelings changed.

_____

_____

_____

_____

Personal Affirmations

Use this section to write down your own affirmations, those that speak to your personal situation. Remember to write in the present tense as if things are happening now.

1.--

2.--

3.--

4.--

5.--

6.

7.

8.

9.

10.

Notes/Reflections

Date_____

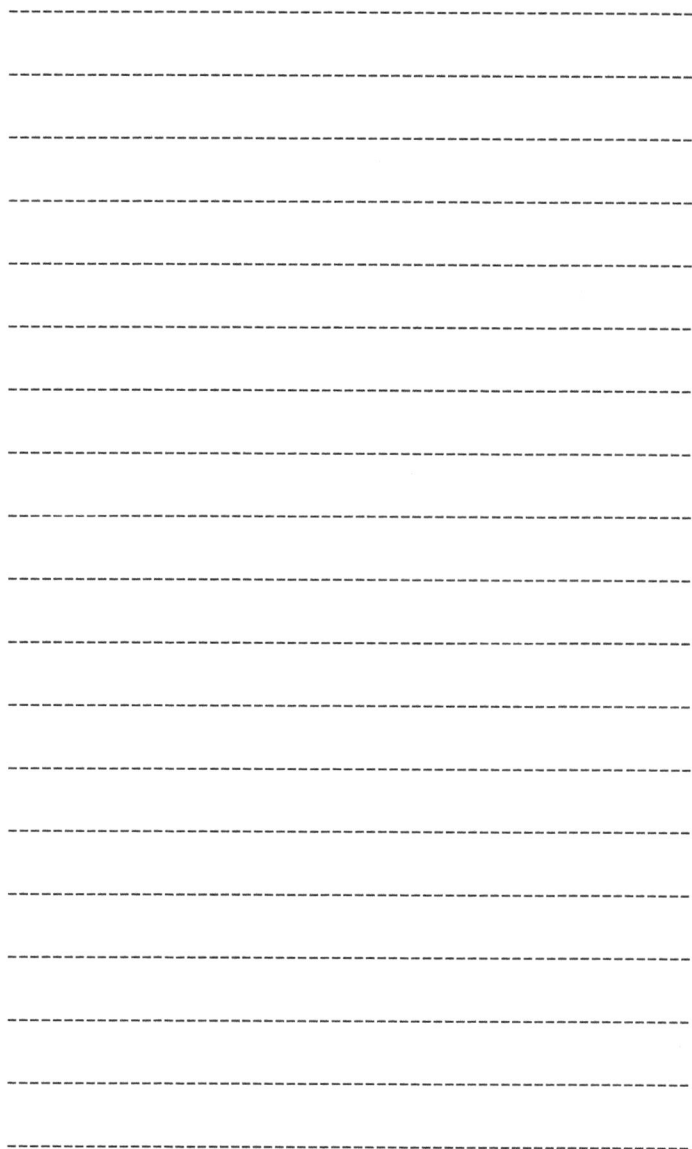

Date_____

Date_____

Date_____

Date_____

Date_____

Date_____

68

Date_____

Date_____

72

Date_____

Date_____

Date_____

Date_____

Date_____

Date_____

Date_____

Date_____

Date_____

Date_____

Date_____

Date_____

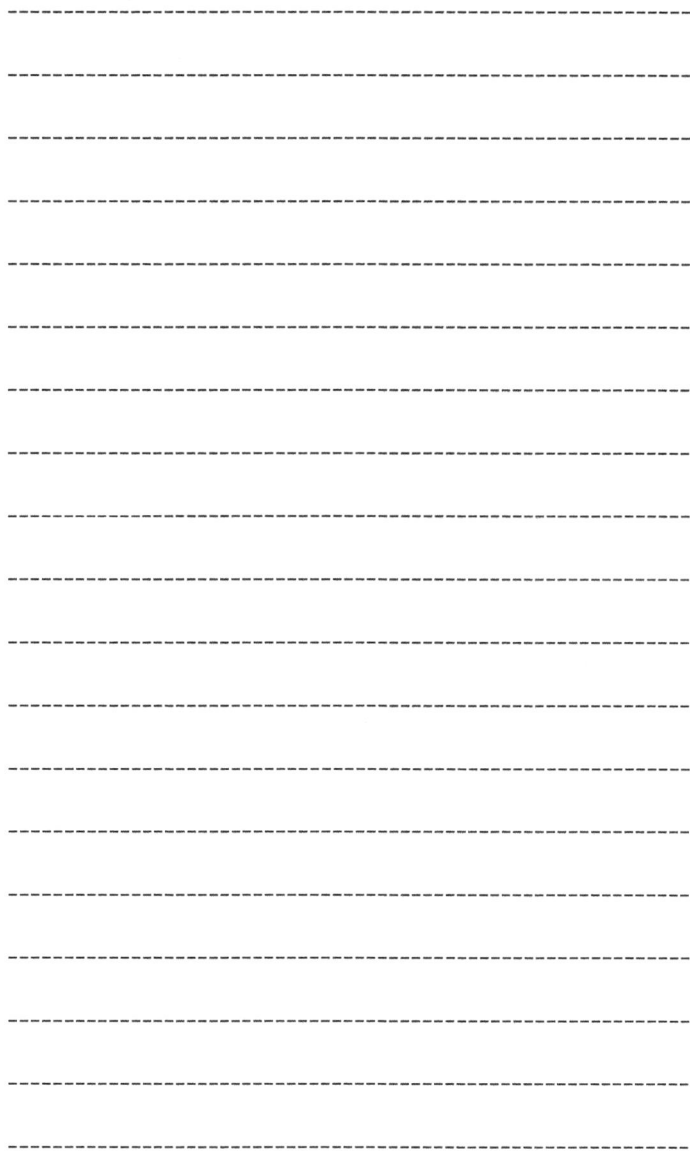

Date_____

Date_____

Date_____

Date_____

Date_____

Date_____

Date_____

Date_____

Date_____

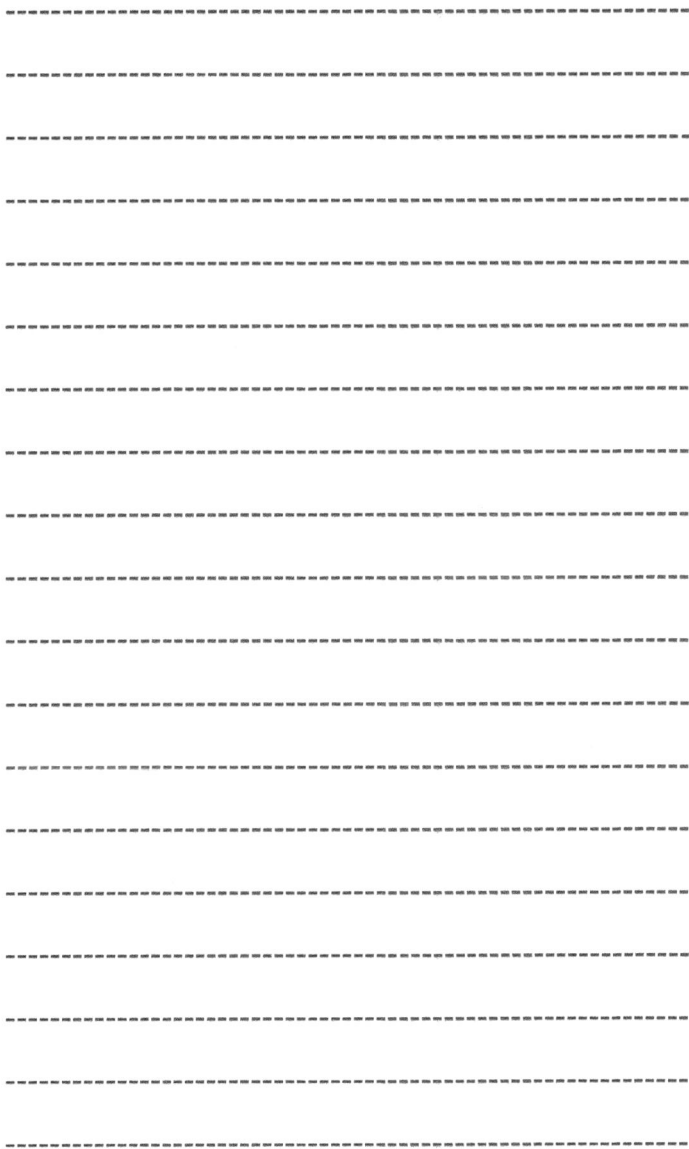

About the Author

Nicole Thomas currently resides in New York, where she works as an HR professional. She holds a BA in psychology and an MS in organizational leadership. She is the author of the books *My View from the Summit (VFS)*, *#Thoughts* and the journal *And for This I Am Grateful.*